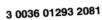

RENEWABLE ENERGY

GLOBAL CITIZENS: ENVIRONMENTALISM

Published in the United States of America by Cherry Lake Publishing
Ann Arbor, Michigan
www.cherrylakepublishing.com

Content Adviser: Michael Rockett MS, Natural resources

Reading Adviser: Marla Conn MS, Ed., Literacy specialist, Read-Ability, Inc.

Photo Credits: © DrimaFilm / Shutterstock.com, cover, 1; © elxeneize / Shutterstock.com, 5; © tchara / Shutterstock.com, 6; © vladee / Shutterstock.com, 8; © You Touch Pix of EuToch / Shutterstock.com, 9; © Robert Lucian Crusitu / Shutterstock.com, 10; © Carmensieta / Shutterstock.com, 13; © Darren Baker / Shutterstock.com, 14; © Lissandra Melo / Shutterstock.com, 15; © Gyuszko-Photo / Shutterstock.com, 16; © urbazon / Shutterstock.com, 19; © Jim Parkin / Shutterstock.com, 20; © A.Punpleng / Shutterstock.com, 23; © Daniel Korzeniewski / Shutterstock.com, 24; © Masa Kato / Shutterstock.com, 26; © Happy Together / Shutterstock.com, 27; © franco lucato / Shutterstock.com, 28

Library of Congress Cataloging-in-Publication Data
Names: Labrecque, Ellen, author.
Title: Renewable energy / Ellen Labrecque.
Description: Ann Arbor : Cherry Lake Publishing, 2017. | Series: Global citizens. Environmentalism | Includes
    bibliographical references and index. | Audience: Grades 4 to 6.
Identifiers: LCCN 2016058616| ISBN 9781634728676 (hardcover) | ISBN 9781634729567 (pdf) |
    ISBN 9781534100459 (pbk.) | ISBN 9781534101340 (hosted ebook)
Subjects: LCSH: Renewable energy sources—Juvenile literature.
Classification: LCC TJ808.2 .L33 2017 | DDC 333.79/4—dc23
LC record available at https://lccn.loc.gov/2016058616

Cherry Lake Publishing would like to acknowledge the work of the Partnership for 21st Century Learning.
Please visit *www.p21.org* for more information.

Printed in the United States of America
Corporate Graphics

ABOUT THE AUTHOR

Ellen Labrecque has written over 100 books for children. She is passionate about being a friend to the environment and taking care of our planet. She lives in Pennsylvania with her husband, Jeff, and her two young "editors," Sam and Juliet. She loves running, hiking, and reading.

TABLE OF CONTENTS

History: Renewable Energy

Environmentalism is a big word. But its meaning is simple. Practicing environmentalism means being a friend of Earth and all its creatures. Environmentalists want to keep our air healthy, our land clean, and our water fresh. They want to take care of our plants and animals by making sure our planet remains a safe place to live. Some environmentalists focus on encouraging people to stop polluting. Others encourage people to **recycle**. One of the most important environmental jobs is to encourage everyone to use **renewable resources** as their energy sources.

The Story of Renewable Energy

Using renewable energy is an example of environmentalism.

Many residents in California and Arizona use solar energy to power their homes.

Biomass is a popular source of renewable energy in Europe.

This is energy from sources that can never be used up, such as the sun and the wind. Most of the world's population uses **nonrenewable resources**—like oil, coal, and gas—to power their cars, heat their homes, and charge their electronic devices. But environmentalists around the world are working every day to change this.

Before the 19th century, all the energy we used was renewable. **Biomass**, used to make fire, is one of the first and oldest forms of renewable energy. Biomass is materials from trees and plants. It is considered renewable because we can always grow more of it. Wind was also an early form of renewable energy. We used wind to power our ships thousands of years ago.

Machines Changed Everything

The Industrial Revolution in the 1800s changed the way we use energy. This was when we started using machines to make things. These machines ran on nonrenewable resources called **fossil fuels**. Fossil fuels can be found below Earth's surface. Digging and drilling for them can harm the environment. Sometimes forests have to be cut down in order to find fossil fuels. When this happens, wild animals lose their homes.

Oil refineries produce pollution.

Researchers believe climate change caused an Arizona park to flood during a monsoon.

Once fossil fuels like oil, coal, and gas are extracted, they need to be **refined** before anyone can use them. Certain studies indicate that the process of refining fossil fuels may be contributing to the extreme weather happening throughout the world. Scientists call this **climate change**. Some scientists believe climate change may be the reason why we are seeing an increase in **droughts** and **monsoons**.

Back to the Basics

Scientists know we have to get back to using renewable

Rock Port, Missouri is the first US city to be completely powered by wind energy.

resources to get our energy. There are several sources of renewable energy: wind, solar (getting energy from the sun), hydropower (getting power from water), and geothermal (getting energy from below Earth's surface). These types of energy are used all over the world, but much more could still be done. Scientists believe we should rely 100 percent on these sources and leave fossil fuels behind forever.

Developing Questions

Environmentalists believe we rely too much on fossil fuels. How can we cut back on this dependence? Why do you think it might be difficult to completely stop using fossil fuels?

A close-ended question is a question that can be answered with a simple yes or no. An open-ended question is one that needs more thought when answering. The questions above are meant to be open-ended questions. They are meant to make you think about ways you can change your habits rather than just answering yes or no.

CHAPTER 2

Geography: Renewable Energy Around the World

Scientists are working around the world to move people away from fossil fuels and toward sources of renewable energy. Some countries do better than others. In the United States, only about 13 percent of our energy use comes from renewable sources, while in Iceland it is almost close to 100 percent!

Iceland

Iceland is a small country next to Greenland and has about 300,000 people living there. It also happens to have 40 active volcanic systems running through it. Iceland gets most of its renewable energy from this volcanic geothermal activity. Geothermal energy comes from heat produced below Earth's

Almost all of Iceland's electricity is produced from renewable energy sources.

This is one of five geothermal plants in Iceland.

Iceland's geothermal energy keeps sidewalks and roads free from ice and snow.

surface. When a volcano becomes active, it spews this energy as liquid rock called magma. If it doesn't produce magma, then this geothermal energy can be converted and used for heating homes and producing electricity. Iceland has five major geothermal plants that make this happen. The country has even used these plants to create heated sidewalks and streets!

Germany

Germany is moving its country toward renewable energy. The country encourages citizens to install **solar panels** on their

Sun Ship is a community in Germany that produces more energy than it consumes.

roofs. These solar panels generate energy for people's houses and also feed into the **energy grid** for the entire country. Germany even has feed-in laws. This means that if people share their solar panel energy with the country, the government pays them money for it. It's an energy win-win.

Gathering and Evaluating Sources

Different types of maps show different things. A political map shows the borders of countries and states. Physical maps show landscape features, such as mountains and rivers. Some maps help tell a story. The map from the Smithsonian magazine helps tell the story of renewable energy. It shows which countries around the world use renewable energy the most and which ones use it the least. Explore this map and discover new information at http://www.smithsonianmag.com/innovation/interactive-mapping-renewable-energy-around-world.

Civics: Everybody Helps

If the world hopes to one day become 100 percent committed to renewable energy use, then everybody—governments, businesses, and individuals—needs to commit to this plan.

The Government's Work for Renewable Energy

Governments around the world have an important job in promoting renewable energy. They establish laws and policies that encourage companies and individuals to use more of it. Governments can do this on a world level, a national level, and a local level.

In 2015, government leaders around the world met to discuss climate change. More than 190 nations gathered in Paris, France, and agreed to cut down on emissions, or the burning of fossil

Over 120 of Apple's retail stores are completely powered by renewable energy.

fuels. The United States pledged to reduce its emissions by 28 percent by 2025.

Businesses Making a Difference

RE100 is an organized effort by companies around the world committed to using renewable energy sources. The technology giant Apple is one of these companies. Ninety-three percent of Apple's facilities—which include its offices, retail stores, and data centers—run on renewable energy. Apple has built solar and wind farms around the world. Solar farms are places that use solar

Texas ranks number one in the United States for its wind energy capacity
and for the number of wind turbines installed.

panels to generate electricity for other people. Wind farms are places that use **wind turbines** to capture wind energy and convert it into electricity for other people. Wind turbines have big rotating blades that sit on top of a tower. When the blades turn from the wind, they connect to a handle inside the tower that is connected to a generator. The generator makes electricity.

Developing Claims and Using Evidence

There are many companies that are committed to using renewable energy. Why might some companies have a difficult time making this same commitment? Using the evidence you find from your local library and the Internet, form an opinion on this subject.

Economics: Funding for Renewable Energy

Governments and private organizations around the world invested $286 billion on renewable energy in 2015. The real investment, though, is saving Earth. What countries did the most for our planet?

China

China invested $102.9 billion into renewable energy in 2015. This money went mostly to solar and wind technologies. In 2016, China began to build the largest solar farm in the world. The farm is equal to the size of 7,000 city blocks. China also has a coastline that is more than 9,000 miles (14,484 kilometers) long. This entire coastline generates wind that can be captured and converted to electricity.

China's electric car industry is also booming.

In 2015, 46 percent of renewable energy in the United States came from hydropower.

United States

The United States invested $44.1 billion in renewable energy in 2015. This is $7 billion more than the previous year. The biggest solar farm investment was in Primm, Nevada. When the city's solar farm is completed, it is expected to power about 80,000 homes. The biggest wind investment was a wind farm in Holt County, Nebraska. It powers about 120,000 homes.

Communicating Conclusions

Before reading this book, did you know about renewable energy? Now that you know more, why do you think this is an important issue? Share your knowledge about renewable energy and the importance of saving our planet. Every week, look up different organizations that support renewable energy. Share what you learn with friends at school or with family at home.

This is a wind and solar power plant in Tahara, a city in Japan.

Japan is slightly smaller than California in land size.

Japan

Japan invested $36.2 billion in renewable energy in 2015.
Japan is just a small island. It has a little less land than the state of
California. This means there is not a lot of space to put solar and
wind farms. Instead, a majority of its renewable energy comes
from offshore wind farms. Offshore wind farms have turbines in
the middle of the water. These farms can collect the wind without
taking up valuable land space.

Many people are needed to install and maintain solar panels.

Renewable Energy Makes Money for People

Renewable energy brings money and jobs into countries. It is estimated that there were more than 7.7 million jobs worldwide in the renewable energy field in 2014. China had the most with 3.4 million jobs, followed by Brazil and the United States. Solar energy provided the most renewable jobs worldwide, with roughly 2.5 million people working in this field.

Taking Informed Action

Do you want to support renewable energy? There are many ways you can get involved and many different organizations you can explore. Here are three to check out:

- *US Energy Information Administration: Learn about how renewable energy is used in the United States.*
- *Green Learning: Find out how to build your own solar oven!*
- *Veggie Van Organization: Discover different ways you can transfer from using fossil fuels to renewable energy.*

Think About It

There are more than 7 billion people living on Earth. It is estimated that by 2050, 9.7 billion people will live here. Population growth and renewable energy are linked together. The more people on our planet, the more people will need fossil fuels to heat their homes and drive their cars. Scientists think all these new people need to understand how they can stop climate change. Providing education about using renewable energy is the first step to a cleaner future. How might learning about renewable energy help stop climate change? Use the data you find to support your argument.

For More Information

FURTHER READING

Challoner, Jack. *Energy*. London: DK Publishing, 2012.

Paleja, Shaker. *Power Up! A Visual Exploration of Energy*. Toronto: Annick Press, 2015.

Spilsbury, Richard, and Louise Spilsbury. *Let's Discuss Energy Resources: Solar Power*. New York: PowerKids Press, 2012.

WEB SITES

Alliant Energy Kids
www.alliantenergykids.com
Lessons on renewable energy help answer questions on the subject.

Green Schools Alliance
www.greenschoolsalliance.org/home
Get your school involved with renewable energy projects.

Wind Energy Foundation
www.windenergyfoundation.org
This is a great place to begin your wind energy research.

GLOSSARY

biomass (BYE-oh-mas) plant matter that can be converted into an energy source

climate change (KLYE-mit CHAYNJ) a change in normal weather patterns over a long period of time

droughts (DROUTS) periods of dry weather

energy grid (EN-er-gee GRID) the place where all energy is stored

environmentalism (en-vye-ruhn-MEN-tuhl-iz-uhm) working to protect the air, water, animals, and plants from pollution and other harmful things

fossil fuels (FAH-suhl FYOOLZ) oil, coal, and gas formed from the remains of animals and plants that died and decayed millions of years ago

monsoons (mon-SOONZ) seasons marked by heavy rains

nonrenewable resources (non-rih-NOO-uh-buhl REE-sors-iz) things of value from the earth, like fossil fuels, that cannot be replaced and can be eventually used up

recycle (ree-SYE-kuhl) to break something down in order to make something new from it

refined (rih-FINED) to be purified or have unwanted matter removed from a substance such as oil

renewable resources (rih-NOO-uh-buhl REE-sors-iz) natural power, such as wind, that will never be used up and can be used again and again

solar panels (SOH-lur PAN-uhlz) materials that form part of a surface and are used to absorb the sun's rays

wind turbines (WIND TUR-buhnz) machines that capture energy from the wind, which eventually is converted to electricity

INDEX